MW00774322

...and then there was Penny

*...and then
there was*

Penny

Audrey Elliott

illustrated by Carl W. Jacobsen

FITHIAN PRESS · SANTA BARBARA, 1998

Published by Fithian Press
A division of Daniel and Daniel, Publishers, Inc.
Post Office Box 1525
Santa Barbara, CA 93102

Book design: Eric Larson

LIBRARY OF CONGRESS CATALOGING-IN-PUBLICATION DATA
Elliott, Audrey, (date)
    And then there was Penny / by Audrey Elliott.
      p.   cm.
    ISBN 1-56474-250-4 (alk. paper)
      1. Dogs—anecdotes. 2. Elliott, Audrey, (date). I. Title
SF426.2.E58   1998
636.8—dc21   97-32024
                                                 CIP

To my parents

Annie Nugent Preston
Warren Wilfred Preston

who taught me to

love and honor God
love and respect people
love and protect animals

Contents

Prologue

MY HEART IS BUBBLING OVER with enthusiasm as I relate to you some of the hundreds of happy hours my pets have given to me. Strangely, though, it was sadness that prompted me to share these precious memories.

Without much warning, my number ten pet, Penny, a jewel who needed polishing, had to be put to sleep. I grieved more than I care to admit, and I dreaded waking up in the morning without the greeting I had come to expect.

In the past, whenever there has been a crisis in my life, I have been able to deal with it positively and often find a hidden blessing beyond the tears.

One night I awoke suddenly thinking that Penny was in distress. Quickly I reached to assure her that all was well, and then realized that it was only a dream. Soon afterward I fell asleep again, and this time my subconscious took me on a more pleasant flight.

As plain as day, I was holding a medium-size, bright blue book in my hand. There were a few gold lines across the cover and part of a sentence: "...and then there was Penny." I leaped out of bed and wrote down the details, fearful that I would not remember them in the morning.

At breakfast I relived my vision of the night before and decided to take action. Hence, you have in hand the proof of my decision, and I can truthfully say that I have never grieved since that important night. The joy of the recollection of such wonderful animals has taken away all my sorrow.

...and then there was Penny

Old Ted

OLD TED WAS MY FIRST LOVE. He was very special; yes, very special indeed. We lived on a farm, so he was an outdoor dog and had his regular duties, like rounding up the cows from pasture at milking time, and maybe watching little piglets to see that they stayed close to their mothers, and even helping my dad when he went hunting groundhogs.

Life was very serene—not much to challenge Old Ted's regular routine—until suddenly little Audrey entered the picture. My mother and dad were a little worried that he might be a bit jealous of a new baby after having all the attention to himself, but such was not the case. He accepted me as another of his responsibilities and was anxiously waiting to care for me whenever I was outside.

Ted was a good-looking dog. He was a medium-size collie, black and tan with long, shiny hair and a white bib under his chin. He kept himself immaculately clean. During the warm weather he was stationed outside and slept close to the house. In the wintertime, when the weather was cold, he spent the nights in the stable with his friends the cows and horses.

Since my mother had not had a wee one in the house for over thirteen years, she had some adjustments to make. She did not even have a baby carriage. My parents bought a very plain black leather "buggy" with quite large wheels, and often I was left in it on the veranda for my morning nap. Dear Ted decided that his main role was to protect me, and therefore, big as he was, he managed with much difficulty to get under that bed on wheels and take up his guardianship of little Audrey. I do not remember it, but I was told that when I was very small, whether awake or sleeping, if anyone put my hand on Ted's soft, silky coat, I would smile even though I would not open my eyes. My love for dogs began at an early age.

I can still remember that baby carriage, as later it provided the ideal place to put my family of dolls, teddy bears, and so on, to bed for the night. Later my dad bought a little wagon for me, and when he moved it in readiness to take me for a ride, guess who was always in it first? Finally there was not room for both of us, but Ted tried to prolong his seniority.

Ted was delighted when I learned to walk, and no one needed to worry that he would let me get in harm's way. My grandmother lived across two small fields, and my dad made a hole in the fence so I could go to her house without traveling on the road. Ted was always at the hole first, both going and coming, so there was no concern about my hither or yon. We wandered over many of the farm areas, sometimes even to the woods, where we watched my dad boil down the sap to make maple syrup. Sometimes we had a nap in the fence corner, but we always came home together, satisfied that neither of us was alone. Ted instilled in me a great trust for dogs, and my love deepened as the years rolled by.

That was when we got our first car, but in no way could we persuade Ted that it was a safe place to be. No such rides for him!

Then came school days. What a nuisance! Of course Ted expected that he would accompany me to the little red schoolhouse, but he had his regular duties at home. I would walk to the nearest farmhouse, where other children joined me for our one and one half miles to our "institution of learning," as we called it. It took my dad a long time to convince Ted to walk with him and me as far as the neighbor's and then leave me and go back with him. Ted soon learned the time of my return, and he would always be waiting for me at the same place where we had parted. Then together we would bounce with joy all the way home. I do not know who was happier to see whom!

Over time I became more interested in playmates, colts, calves, and the menagerie of farm animals, and I do not seem to recall when dear old Ted went away. Just as well! As usual, Mother and Dad handled the situation wisely.

Major

MAJOR WAS A DISPLACED DOG and, being older when he came to us, he had considerable adjusting to do. Some friends of ours owned him through his first two years and then found that they could not keep a dog. Knowing that my dad always took in strays, they contacted him and, true to form, he brought Major to our home. Major found it difficult to accept the change but, after three times away to where he used to live and three times back, he settled into his new way of life.

Major was a handsome dog. He was a purebred medium-size collie, orange in color with white markings. He had the carriage of a show dog, and we wondered if for that reason he had been named Major.

Major arrived while I was boarding at school away from home, so only in the holiday months did we find that we belonged together. He was a faithful watch dog, ever ready to remember his duties with the cattle, and was truly admired by all who knew him.

In earlier days someone had built a swing in our front

yard. It was made of wood, shaped like a boat, and seated four people. It hung from four long iron rods and was capable of swinging away up into the wild blue yonder. Major found that he enjoyed swinging, and when anyone approached that particular piece of equipment he would be the first to be in one of the seats and showed his pleasure with squeals of joy or even a few barks. Sometimes, when there was no one outside and we heard excited barking, we would discover the dog in the swing all alone, trying his best to invite someone to join him for a little excitement.

Another one of Major's unusual summer pastimes deserves special mention. Often we would buy a dozen duck eggs from our neighbor and put them under one of our clucking hens to hatch. After the little ducklings were able to walk around and the mother hen had decided that they did not belong in the chicken family, we would take them to a little coop where, by the light of a coal-oil lantern, they would be warm and soon grow up and venture into the yard. Major's whole nature seemed to change. He was intrigued! He had never seen little two-legged unbalanced bodies walking around. His wheels were turning. They surely needed a mother, and they had no fear of him. With his new interest, he would check on them in the morning, perhaps several times, and later in the day it was a common sight to see Major walking slowly across the grass followed by a line, sometimes single file, of little ducklings quacking in glee. They did not know what their mother would have looked like, so they decided to take a chance on whomever was at hand. Sometimes they would pause in the warmth of the sunshine, and Major would lie down and let one or more wee ducklings crawl up on his back and even sleep briefly, their little heads tucked under their wings. Others would cuddle close to his warm body, and sometimes he would put his paw gently over them.

They were truly in the security of the dog's embrace.

Even full-grown ducks continued this unique friendship. Major seemed overjoyed that he had found a new responsibility in his later years and looked forward to a new duck family every springtime.

Sarah Geraldine, a.k.a. Sally

EVER SINCE I CAN REMEMBER, I wished for a little dog—one that I could cuddle and take with me wherever I went. Do you believe in miracles? Well, I do. My dad arranged to get a toy fox terrier puppy for his eight-month-old grandson, and he could not resist the temptation. He brought home two puppies, a black-and-white male and a white-and-black female. After a few days, the black-and-white one went to his new home, and our whole household was overjoyed to keep the white-and-black one.

Well, that little two pounds of activity needed a name. My mother decided to give a party for my teenage friends with a contest to name the dog. Everyone had to submit a name. My brother-in-law was to bring his family's puppy for a reunion, and he promptly suggested the name Sarah. Other names included Trixie, Buster, Jerry or Geraldine (suggested by my friend Gerald), Spot, Happy, Rosie (by my friend Rose), Max, Christopher (to be shortened to Chris), Patsy, and several others. Of course, some had to be eliminated because they were unsuitable for a girl dog; but finally the decision was unanimous to accept Sarah Geraldine and call her Sally for short. The two puppies were happy to be reunited at the party, and after a boisterous play session they retired to nap—together—on Sally's cushion on the sitting room sofa. Order was restored and lunch was served.

Since Sally was my first small dog, full of pep and enthusiasm but also scared of everything around her, it was necessary to find a way to give her confidence. Can you imagine a puppy with people on every side and feet, feet, feet everywhere? I tried hard to relieve her of all fear, so our first lesson together was for me to teach her complete trust. She learned where to find water, food, protection and, above all, kindness. Every day there was something new to learn or relearn, and she responded very quickly to a small treat and, yes, hated the tone of voice that accompanied the words "bad doggie." Housebreaking was very easy, as we went outside quite often and always made a "happy" fuss after her duties were done, then quickly went inside so that she would learn the pattern. After the first month we had all learned a lot, with much more to come.

Sally was happy with the individual attention and accepted her surroundings without hesitation. She was still only when asleep and could jump over the moon, so to speak. She was smart in every way and learned very quickly to roll her eyes to pretend she was sorry for any mistakes before a correction or reprimand could be given. That way no one could be very cross, naturally.

Sally loved outdoor life in the summertime. She did not enjoy the snow, but if she begged to go to the barn with my dad, he would put her in a basket and carry her.

Spoiled? Well, not exactly. In the barn she found mice occasionally, and she mastered the art of catching them, and with one squeeze only she would deposit her prey at the feet of the first person she could find. Thus she earned the title of "best mouser."

One time my mother received an invitation to a community event in the area where she had grown up. It was a daytime program with an opportunity to meet others paying tribute to their birthplace and ancestors. We decided to take Mother to meet acquaintances of long ago and share in their fellowship, and Sally went along for the ride. A couple who had known some of my mother's family invited us to their home for supper. I explained that we had our dog along, and they were delighted to include her also. Now for an embarrassing moment.

Scarcely had we arrived at the couple's house, been

royally welcomed to their lovely country home, commented on the mirror-like shine of their hardwood floor, when Sally took off at full speed, slipping, falling, picking herself up and starting over—again and again and again. Do you get the picture? The man of the house asked for an explanation of her conduct, and hesitatingly I suggested that on some occasions I would venture that she might suspect a mouse. The hostess hastened to assure us that a mouse was something they seldom saw, but I had my doubts, especially when Sally took up a very watchful position beside the piano. Conversation continued with much reminiscing, and then suddenly Sally made a wild dash and, despite much sliding, caught a mouse, gave it her special squeeze and deposited it at the mister's feet.

At that time there were no clothes dryers. Everyone had a clothesline, and our clothes were very soft and fluffy after being blown dry by the wind and sun. One day my mother noticed that a corner of a bedspread that was on the line had been damaged. She had a suspicion, but no proof. A week or so later, one whole sleeve was missing from a long-sleeved nightgown. She looked rather askance at Sally, but the dog was quick to lower her head, roll her eyes and—you guessed it—my mother said, "I must raise that pole under the clothesline to push it up higher."

Sally grew older and not quite so mischievous, but she never gave up having new brainstorms. The church we attended was on our farm, about the length of a city block from our house. One Sunday, to her dismay, Sally found that there was no one at home. After a few sniffs, I presume, she figured out where we were, so she meandered to the church. The door was open and she heard the voice of the minister preaching, so she entered and stopped in her tracks. So did the preacher. Then he said, "We have a late arrival." I was in the choir, not because I could sing, but because my age group was holding forth that day. The choir loft was at the front of the sanctuary with a railing in front of the singers. Sally sized up the situation, trotted up the aisle, up the steps, and along the railing, sniffing as she went. When she got to me she squatted down and crawled under the railing. The minister completed his sermon with no more interruptions.

Then I was married, fully expecting to take Sally along with me—but my dad had other ideas. He reasoned that Sally would be better where she was, familiar with her surroundings, and I could always train and love another pup. Sally visited often, but happily she returned to her master when the visits were over.

Mickey and Trixie

FOR OUR FIRST WEDDING anniversary my husband thought he should buy me a dog. Good idea!

We were driving north out of Toronto and noticed a sign: KENILWORTH KENNELS, SPECIALIZING IN POMERANIANS. I would have settled for any breed, but since Pomeranians are a long-haired variety, we reasoned that they would do well in the wintertime. We stopped to see what the Kenilworth Kennels had to offer and immediately fell in love with a rusty-blond male who was already named Mickey. He had a curly duster-like tail that wagged constantly, and he was immediately attracted to us. With all the confidence in the world, he was ready to go. He was slow in adjusting to the automobile, but without incident we arrived at home with a very lively pet.

Mickey knew nothing about life beyond the confines of a kennel. With several others, he had shared a small yard and a long adjoining lane, where much running and playing seemed to satisfy some six or seven dogs of various ages.

Changes were in store at Elliott's Farm. When Mickey discovered there were no walls to confine him, he went crazy-wild, going at his highest speed in small circles, then widening into larger circles—here there and everywhere—until he nearly dropped from exhaustion.

To say the least, he was in need of water, some nourishing food, and was ready to settle for the night in his new surroundings. He was about four months old and already in control.

At dawn the next morning we realized that we had an early riser. Before any people were up, Mickey had visited four bedrooms and was aware of five adults in his new family. When he became better acquainted with the family members he would visit each one every morning, jumping on the bed, carefully sniffing to be sure he was welcome and, if so, giving a wet lick to someone's eyelid. If that did not produce results he would draw his paw softly under the lower lid to open one's eye to be certain that whoever it was would understand that it was time to greet a new day.

Shortly after breakfast that first morning I took Mickey for a walk, introducing him to various places he could visit again at leisure. Then I went inside, intending to return in a few minutes—but not few enough, it seemed. For I found that Mickey had ventured as far as the hen house, and hens were flying and scattering as fast as they could to escape the barking intruder. The rooster, in particular, did not approve of Mickey's impudence and flew at him, pecking him wherever he found a suitable spot, even pulling out some of his beautiful hair in small and even large wisps. I heard the yelping and went to investigate, and I could have cried. The rooster had caused what I might have spent days to accomplish. Mickey knew where to go for help, climbing into my arms and uttering low growls of anger. Until his dying day he came to me in joy or in sorrow. Bonding had happened, thanks to the rooster.

Sometimes Mickey and I would go to bring the cows from the pasture to the stable for milking. This was a lot of fun because he was so quick and the cows could not keep track of him. Was he behind them, in front of them, or had he disappeared by running underneath one or more of them? We would have needed a movie camera to record his dexterity. He would not go on this mission with anyone except me. The menfolks did not warrant his support.

Then a change developed. My husband decided to move his business to a village about fifteen miles away. We rented a house, but I would be assisting in the office and Mickey would often be left alone at home. He did not approve, and it became noticeable as he lost his appetite and then much weight. He also lost his happy nature, and he would cry real tears until sometimes we would find him completely soaking wet. He was homesick, missing so much space and lonesome for his many animal friends.

We had an idea to try to get him a companion, and returned to the kennel whence he had come. We settled on a fully matured female of the same breed but a deep, rusty orange in color. She had never been away from the kennel, and she acted shy as well as very fearful. Her hair was shorter than Mickey's, soft and silky, and we named her Trixie. Mickey was interested; Trixie was frightened. Maybe they recognized each other, maybe not; we were never sure. But Mickey accepted her and promptly trained her in the ways of the household.

Our neighbors two doors down the street were an older couple who were devoted dog lovers. Mickey and Trixie soon learned how welcome they were to visit these

shut-ins, and at every opportunity they made a call, sometimes even remaining there until I came home from work.
They recognized the sound of our car driving by and understood the hours for mealtimes, and no one, no matter
how attentive, could have kept them from scampering
home on their own at these times.

Sometimes it was necessary for us to go on business to
a city about forty miles away, and when we did the dogs
always accompanied us. If we happened to be there at
mealtime, we liked to eat at a Chinese restaurant where
we enjoyed the food and the service. Everyone was so
friendly there! One day, unexpectedly, we were detained
longer than usual, and it was very cold—too cold to leave
Mickey and Trixie in the car while we dined. Those were
times before there were any ordinances excluding dogs
from eating places, so I stepped inside and asked our Chinese host if it would be possible for us to bring the dogs
inside while we ate if we promised to keep them under the
table and made sure they were well behaved. Mr. Chung
was delighted, so in we came.

We were seated at a round booth so that the dogs
could sit on a bench beside us. What a wonderful experience it was, and how proud we were of our darling pets!
When our dinners were served, can you believe it, they
brought two small dishes with chopped food for the extra
hungry mouths we had along. That was the only time we
ever took the dogs into the dining room, but always after
that we were given two doggie bags to take home with
Mr. Chung's compliments. Maybe that was the introduction of the doggie bag era.

Another change was forthcoming. We bought a house
and would soon be moving with our canary, white
pussycat, and two dogs. We had to bid our wonderful
neighbors goodbye, assuring them of periodic visits from

their Pomeranian friends. But what a joy! Our new property had a fenced back yard with a vegetable garden behind it. Anytime the gate was left open during the produce season, Trixie would steal an onion and eat it all by herself—dirt and all—much to the dismay of Mickey, who simply could not stand the smell of her.

Soon after we were settled we discovered that Trixie would become a mother. What excitement! In due time she presented us with two puppies, a male and a female, one to be a blondie and the other a rusty brown like Trixie. What fun we were to have!

The puppies were about the size of mice, with eyes tightly closed but already able to make sounds almost like the mews of baby kittens. Trixie was a wonderful mother. She was very careful to keep her babies bathed every morning with her trusty tongue and again with additional licks often throughout the day. She promptly let Mickey know to keep his distance, but when the puppies were able to walk around and see a little, he began his duties of assisting with the morning baths, trading puppies with Trixie every other day. Truly, it was an education to watch how methodically they performed, and a delight to see how these parents wanted to share their family with people. Trixie had the puppies "potty-paper" trained before they were a month old.

The dog family had their bedroom in the basement beside the furnace, where they would always be warm; but they were true pets and wanted to be with people whenever possible. We named the pups Linda and Louie, and it was interesting to see how quickly they learned their names.

Picture with me an evening in the living room. My husband was resting on the sofa, reading the paper, which he had missed earlier in the day, and Mama and Papa dogs were together in one chair, each with one eye on their offspring. The pups were playing roly-poly on the rug, learning to box a bit, talking to each other in their particular language, when suddenly Linda barked—her first bark. It startled us, to be sure, and my husband pushed his paper to his stomach as together we watched Louie try to show off his bark also. No such luck; that was going to take practice and more time. But all of a sudden the playing stopped. Louie looked around everywhere. He spied the newspaper on my husband's lap, and you have three guesses what he did next. He had no problem springing up to the sofa, and we agreed that he was already a smart dog. He knew how to take advantage of a situation, whatever it might be.

Then came Christmas. It was such fun to have a tree in the house. We found it necessary to keep the pups out of the living room, as they were certain that unwrapping the parcels would provide lots of amusement. As I have already said, the dogs all slept in the basement, but we left the door open to the kitchen. A swing-door divided the kitchen and dining room, so they were not allowed the run of the house until we were all up in the morning. A few days after Christmas, however, I said to my husband, "It sounds to me like the pups are in the living room." He assured me he had closed the kitchen doors, but had he?

We ventured to look downstairs. The living room was a shambles. The snow skirt from under the tree was scattered in small pieces all over two rooms; the top layer from a box of chocolates was missing; a napkin, part of a luncheon gift set, had been the object of a tug of war; and we could almost see an expression on both pups that said, "Yes, we did it ourselves." And all the doors to the kitchen *were* closed.

Days later we found the answer. Louie would stand on his hind legs and lean against the swing-door; Linda would run full speed across the kitchen, hit the door with all her weight, and they could both get through on the swing. They often tried a repeat performance, but we made other plans.

Then came time to part with our darling baby dogs. Both were sold. Louie was gone, but Linda awaited the homecoming of a young couple who had bargained for her. We were replacing the backyard fence with green lattice work, and the veranda floor was to be painted the same color. To save time and energy, I decided to spread the lath boards on the veranda, put the paint in a flat basin and attack my job with a wide paintbrush. But I had not counted on Linda's assistance. I did not see her arrive on the scene; she appeared from nowhere. She sat down in the basin of dark green paint, then decided to move closer to me, and her tail was really a wagging paintbrush. To say the least, I had a change of occupation. No way could I wipe away all the paint. Much hair had to be trimmed from Linda and, you guessed it, the new owners phoned just then to arrange a pick-up. I persuaded them to allow me overnight to make Linda more presentable. Fortunately, they loved her—paint and all!

Still more changes were in store. Trixie gave us two more litters of pups, each more dear than the last, then she peacefully went to sleep one night and did not awaken. Also, my dad was fatally injured in an accident, and my mother came to live with us. We had an opportunity to purchase a house that we had long admired, and in due time two friends who had lived with us as well as myself, my husband, Mom, plus Mickey, Tabby, our white cat, and her four kittens all moved to the new surroundings. This proved to be a wonderful place for animals to play. In one area there was a "roundabout" from dining room to living room to den and hall and then back through the living room again. Can you see the procession of dog and cat around the circle, followed by four playful kittens sometimes pushed out of the way? Rough treatment for small fry!

Mickey, like most dogs, was very fond of ice cream. I taught him to hold a cone between his front paws and turn it around with every lick. He would never spill a drop, not even on the living room rug. To show his appreciation he would look around at everyone in sight and close his eyes. That was the closest he could come to a smile with his mouth full of ice cream.

One day I had Mickey with me at the county fair. We were walking down the midway when the crowd came off the grandstand. To prevent Mickey from being trampled, I picked him up and carried him, holding him close to my body. I did not notice, though he did, a lady very near us enjoying a big ice cream cone. With one motion only, Mickey removed the whole scoop of ice cream, and with one gulp swallowed it. The lady was irate. I offered to buy her another, but it seemed that only the one Mickey had consumed would satisfy her. Sorry, lady, we did our best!

Mickey was getting older. He was still very alert and energetic, but his hair was losing its beautiful orange cast. I watched him more carefully. One morning I was making pies for dinner and I felt Mickey scratching on my leg. I looked down, and he seemed okay. I said, "Mama can't hold you now, her hands are covered with flour." But he persisted, scratching my leg again, so I washed my hands and picked him up. He gasped, and I took him to the door for a breath of cold, fresh air. He reached up and gave me a "goodbye" kiss, gasped, and was gone. Like I said, the bonding was always there, in joy or in sorrow, thanks to the rooster.

Perky

MY, WHAT A LONELY HOME it was after Mickey was gone, leaving his Pomeranian influence to linger throughout the household. I was distressed at losing my pet and a bit uneasy about broaching the subject of a new dog. What a decision it would be! Yet nobody talked about a replacement. Then came plans for a holiday weekend in the Niagara district.

The morning we were to leave, I scanned the Toronto paper and actually clipped the column of "Pups for Sale." The name "chihuahua" caught my eye. I had never heard of that breed. I had already decided that I did not want another long-haired dog—but what was a chihuahua? Anyway, I carefully put the newspaper clipping in my purse, and off we went on our holiday.

Mental telepathy was at work. As we were driving along my husband said, "How about looking for a pup while we are away?" I could hardly believe my ears! Then I admitted that I had a suggestion in my purse, and I produced the newspaper clipping. I mentioned the "chihuahua," but he didn't know what it was either, so we decided to investigate. The address given in the clipping was very near the highway we were traveling, so we found the place with no problem.

Yes, the people said, they had two puppies—chihuahuas, six weeks old, a male and a female. Like all puppies, they were darling to me; but these were exceptional. Which would we choose? Neither, at this particular time, as we would be staying at the Brock Hotel, where no pet would be welcome. Instead we bargained for a pup, either pup; if the owners found a place for one of them before we came back the next day, we would be satisfied with whichever was left.

We enjoyed our short holiday, but we could hardly wait to start back and pick up our chihuahua. I couldn't even sleep for happiness, and we lost no time in setting out in the morning. We learned that the female chihuahua had meanwhile been sold, so ours would be the male, and we took him home with us that very day.

I was so anxious that our new pet would bond quickly to me that I took my pajama top from my luggage and wrapped the little bundle of joy for his first car ride. He seemed not to be lonely, and seemed to like the car. He also liked the motherly smell of his coverlet, so we were well on our way, brimming over with such a good feeling of accomplishment.

We picked up a passenger in Toronto, and all three people and the one pup rode together in the front seat of our car. The wee doggie investigated the new lady who joined us. She was okay, so it was nap time. Every now and then he awoke to be startled by the brilliance of a pin on our passenger's suit, and he would try to bite it and pull it off her coat. Of course, puppies have a habit of biting anything and everything, and so this could have been expected.

When we arrived home we were greeted by my mother, who exclaimed, "So, you *did* get a new dog!" Mothers have an extra sense, and she fully expected what had already taken place.

We shared a driveway with neighbors who had a toy bull terrier called Happy. Even he surmised something and came to call with a sniff-sniff here and a sniff-sniff there, and we all played together in the yard. Happy got excited and had to find a place to squat. That gave the nameless new arrival an idea, so he tried it too. Ever after, that was hallowed ground, and there were no problems about bathroom privileges. Lucky for all of us!

Then came the naming, and that was easy. With such wide-awake eyes, and being so quick in every way, what name could be better than Perky? So Perky Elliott had arrived with full dog honors and already had all our friends and neighbors vying to be his favorite.

But what about bedtime? Perky was tired; his day had been quite exhausting. I had a dog basket, which I quickly brought out of storage, placed on the floor beside our bed, and lined with a hand-knit green-and-yellow afghan. It did look inviting, and with the extra temptation of an arrowroot biscuit, Perky arranged the folds of the afghan to dog satisfaction, ate one half of the biscuit, and gave up without a whimper. Leaving a whole or half biscuit uneaten became a habit of his. It could be put to good use later, if necessary.

In the morning Perky seemed confused. There were no familiar places or objects, no mother, no sister—nothing was the same. But his attitude seemed to be, "Oh, well, let's try something new," and there were fantastic new opportunities and new friends everywhere.

Training days lay ahead. Experience had taught me that dogs like to learn one word at a time, so we worked together on "car," "leash," and "water" (and what fun it was to upset the water dish!). We also taught Perky some "no" words. He learned that the doorbell meant company, and after a little while he thought he might make friends if he ran upstairs to fetch a leftover biscuit from his basket and toss it up in the air. He won lots of praise that way when he mastered the art of catching the biscuit.

One day a cousin came by to show off her baby, who was about six months old. She was something different, from Perky's point of view. She sat on a quilt in the middle of the living room; strangely, she could not walk, but just looked around. And she had a biscuit. Not to be outdone, Perky remembered that he had a bone in the kitchen, and he decided to show it off. We adults were engaged in conversation when we suddenly noticed that the baby's biscuit had disappeared, replaced in her fist and mouth by Perky's bone. And guess where the biscuit had gone?

In our town we picked up our mail each morning at the post office. Perky was always waiting to go for a walk, at first with the humiliation of a leash, but later, because of good behavior, he trotted along beside me without restraint. He was well known and admired by everyone on our street.

In those days, small dogs were allowed in grocery stores. On our way home we often stopped to buy something. Perky soon found that the manager of one shop tried to win his favor by treating him to arrowroot cookies. Then we learned something: this doggie had discriminating taste. There were at that time four companies who sold similar cookies packaged in similar cartons; but Perky found that two were palatable to him and two were not. The news was passed along to the salesman who took orders for the store, and he interviewed me to see if he could use a picture of Perky on an advertising billboard with the caption "Even a dog knows the difference." Unfortunately, it didn't work out.

But Perky was not always so lucky. Do you know about skunks? Well, we do! One night we had been to a very special party, all dressed up in our best clothes. It was late when we returned, and I let Perky out for his bedtime "tree-tree"; it was then that I smelled a skunk, and a moment later I heard Perky yelping and scratching furiously at the door. I let him in, and he ran all around the living room wiping his face on the carpet. Bad news! His eyes were almost closed by the stinging spray from the skunk, and out of pity I picked him up to console him. Worse news! I suddenly realized what my clothes would smell like, so I put Perky down; but he immediately ran upstairs and jumped into bed with my mother. The worst news! Mom called out, "Audrey! Come and get this dog," which I did as fast as possible. Then I realized we needed help. Despite the hour, I phoned our neighbor, who was a doctor, to see if he had something for Perky's eyes. He came on the run with eye drops to relieve the pain and a can of tomato juice for a bath to relieve the smell. Peace was finally restored after a couple of days; but it was short-lived, as it turned out.

We were staying at the cottage, which Perky dearly loved. He was captain of the motorboat, standing at the bow and barking at the neighboring campers as he rode along. Every morning he would run out to the end of the dock, where he would stand and watch the little fish darting about for what seemed like hours. It always ended up with Perky falling head first into the lake. We surmised that watching the fish made him dizzy; but whatever the cause, he had his dunk this way every day.

One day Perky left part of his dinner in his dish on the veranda. We had gone for a car ride, and when we returned there was a skunk eating the remains of the meal. Perky was enraged and came running down the steps to the cottage. The skunk reacted in his usual way before scampering off into the night. More tomato juice—and more on the shelf, just in case.

A year passed, and again we went to the cottage. It was Saturday afternoon, and I was preparing for a houseful of company on Sunday. I had made two fresh cherry pies and set them on the windowsill to cool. Groceries had been ordered, and I decided that Perky and I would go to the store to pick them up. We were gone about ten minutes, and returned with three bags of groceries. I took one load down the fifteen or so steps to the cottage, and left the kitchen door propped open while I went back for the rest. My neighbor was at that moment greeting guests whom I knew very well, and I stopped to welcome them to Oak Lake Campground, then returned to my groceries. Perky preceded me down the steps this time, and started barking as we approached the cottage. Before I realized what had happened, Perky had discovered a skunk, probably the same one that had visited a year ago, and he chased it through the propped-open door and into the kitchen. As soon as the skunk saw that he was cornered, he used his only means of protection and sprayed the whole room, then took up a watchful position under the kitchen sink.

Luckily the dog was safe, but the stove, table, sink, counters, and walls were wet with skunk spray. I no longer recall how I got rid of our unwelcome guest—and I'm glad I don't. Just then my nephew came home, and I asked him to take the pies and put them somewhere away from that awful smell. This he did, and I promptly forgot about them.

I spent most of the night washing the whole kitchen,

even the floor, with tomato juice and then hot, sudsy water. At breakfast the next morning I suddenly remembered
the pies and asked my nephew where he had taken them.
"I put them upstairs, in my dresser drawer," he said. Fortunately, they were okay; no additional flavor had been
added.

Fortunately, too, that was the end of our skunk epi-
sodes!

.

Perky was a very affectionate dog and was especially fond of my mother. Mom had a weak heart and rested on the living room sofa almost every afternoon. Perky could hardly wait. As soon as she was comfortable, he stationed himself in the back bend of her knees until she was ready to move. Mom died very suddenly on February 29—a special day in every way. We had her in her walnut casket at the house, and every time Perky went near, he jumped up to get in with her. One evening, after all the callers had gone, I lifted him up to be with her. He sized up the situation, but never again begged to get any closer than the floor at her feet.

Mother was buried on March 3, a cold day, about twelve miles from where we lived. We left Perky at home during the funeral. Then, on Mother's Day, early in the morning Perky and I took flowers to the cemetery. Mind you, he had never been to the cemetery before. But when I reached the grave, about seventy-five yards from the car, he was already sitting quietly at Mother's feet. How did he know? In later years, whenever we visited the cemetery Perky's reaction was always the same. He loved deeply, and remembered well.

Perky was quite widely traveled. He rode with us three times to Florida, once to California, and once to the Canadian west. As we were driving along the highway in woodsy northern Michigan, I spotted two fawns resting on the shoulder of the road. It was such an unusual sight that I suggested we back up so everyone could see them. Perky spotted something worth chasing, so I let him out of the car and with great glee he chased the fawns into the woods. Then came an awful yelp for help. Perky came running at full speed, with Mama Deer close behind. We opened the car door and Perky leaped to safety with no trouble.

Once in Florida we managed to rent a motel room at the end of the property, behind which, beyond a fence, was a vacant field. Perky was soon very much at home, running through the field to his heart's content. If he wanted out at night, we would let him out alone. When it was time for him to return, I could go to the door and call "Perk!" and he would come on the run, showing his good training.

Well, about daylight one morning Perky was awakened by the sound of "Perk!" called from outside. I couldn't believe my ears, either, but it was a mockingbird calling "Perk!" as clearly as I could. Naturally Perky answered. This early-morning wakeup call continued for the remainder of our vacation.

Back home to familiar surroundings was always welcome. One night when Perky was outside for his pre-bedtime run at the back of our house, he begged quickly to come in. He could not close his mouth. It was as wide open as it could be, and on examination I found a bone— a T-bone with the point anchored in the roof of his mouth. I tried every way to remove it, but at eleven o'clock I called our wonderful vet, twelve miles away, who said "bring him as quickly as you can." I'm certain I broke all the speed limits, and anyone would while hearing whimpers all the way. The vet had the door open and I gathered Perky in my arms, but as soon as Perky smelled the hospital he jumped from my arms and dislodged the bone. The vet and I settled for coffee.

But all too soon Perky began to show his age and the effects of his wonderful life. At that time there was road construction going on everywhere in front of our home, and of course Perky had to supervise several times a day. The highway was being lowered, and soil was piled up wherever there was space. I began to notice a tenderness in Perky's feet, and our trusty vet diagnosed his problem as some kind of poisoning from contaminated soil dug up from deep underground. We had to treat his four sore feet every morning, but there was no cure—only prevention of a worse condition. Perky was an excellent patient, so grateful for the balm that eased his discomfort. Our vet suggested that boots would be a good idea, and he gave me a piece of soft deerskin, from which I made boots complete with laces around the tops. Perky loved his boots, and kissed me every time he went outside. They protected him from rain, mud, and even snow; and although he had once dearly loved to play in the snow, it seemed that those days were now behind him.

One night when Perky came in at bedtime he had only three boots. We talked about it together, and in the morning I put on his three boots, showed him his one bare foot, and together we went outside. Perky led the way, with me following closely. He took me to the fence where his lost boot was caught on a wire. Order was soon restored with thanksgiving.

But I could see that Perky's condition was worsening, and I tried daily to prepare myself for the inevitable. In just one week his eyesight went, and he began to make mistakes he had never made before. Then one day I had an errand across the street, and I left Perky asleep in a chair. When I returned he raised his head, but I could tell he was weak. I got a soft sheet, folded it in quarters, and wrapped him in it. I raised his little body over my shoulder, said a silent prayer, and held him close until he slumped in my arms.

Farewell, Perky dear.

Joker

A LONG TIME AGO, when I was a little girl, my mother often planned a treat for me in the afternoon. She knew what I enjoyed the most.

In our parlor—what would nowadays be called the living room—there was a pretty basket that held what we called a scope and views. Today the scope would be known as a stereopticon, and the views were pictures in black and white, some in sepia tones, and a few in full color. We put the pictures in the scope and held it to our eyes, and we could see the views in three dimensions, giving us the feeling we were traveling to great cities or enjoying beautiful scenery in faraway places. There were two views that I always saved until the very last: one was of the blue ocean surrounding the Hawaiian Islands; the other showed a grove of orange trees in California. After looking at them, I would say to my mother, "I want to go there to live."

Finally my dream came true. I sold my home, packed some treasures in a U-Haul trailer, and drove across the continent to the Pacific Ocean. Now, how does this story fit into a book about dogs? I could imagine a home in a busy city, renting out extra rooms to boarders, and having a small, devoted dog for my very own companion.

And so Santa Barbara, California, was the answer. Soon I had my home and two fine gentleman boarders; all that remained was to get a dog. My boarders had no objection, so I began watching the ads in the local newspaper. In a very short time I found some chihuahua–Manchester terrier mix puppies advertised, and all three of us went together to investigate.

There were four puppies, the pride and joy of their mama. The lady of the house loved them all; the mother dog was watchful and attentive; and we were all enthralled. But they were too young to be taken away as yet. But I was so elated I could hardly wait, and decided to make my choice now. One was chocolate brown, one a real blond, and two in between, like a plain tan and brindle mix. I rather liked the brindle mix, but as the puppies came nearer to study us strangers, the little tan one came very close to me, and I picked him up. He promptly went to sleep in my hands. It would be a difficult choice, I could see.

After that we headed home again, all three of us gloating with satisfaction and anticipation of that day three weeks hence when we would have an addition to our household. Those three weeks dragged by very, very slowly. We phoned to make an appointment to purchase our pup, and when we arrived we found the same happy family. The pups had developed nicely, but were still under the watchful care of their loving mother. I chose and paid for the brindle mix, and then little mister tan took over the scene. He leaped from the basket, went running, jumping, and even attempted a somersault. Apparently he had chosen me, and I could not resist. So with three people's hearts and one puppy heart beating with excitement, we started for home.

There is a door chime on our front door, and when it is opened it plays "Happy Days Are Here Again," and truer words were never spoken—or, in this case, played instrumentally—for we were indeed a happy gang as we entered.

But our puppy was confused. Where was his mother, his playmates? Even his sleeping basket was nowhere to be found. But the people were friendly—almost too friendly. Everyone wanted him at the same time. As he sized up the situation, it seemed okay after all, and then all of a sudden he was tired and fell fast asleep in a few seconds. He was close beside a warm body on the sofa and felt very welcome.

Someone said, "What shall we call him?" We thought of several suitable names, and I recall saying that I had once known a dog called Joker. One of the boarders laughed and remarked how suitable that name would be, for already our pup had proven to be quite a joker. By the time our new arrival awoke, he had become Joker Elliott, and he was soon to be master of the whole domain.

Nap time, however, was brief; he stirred a bit and awoke. Very gently I picked him up, and we went outside. Evidently he had not been exposed to green grass before, and he thought it was lots of fun. It even tickled his tummy and, oh yes, maybe it would be a good idea to squat in that soft grass. He was quick to remember the delight of space and a yard full of grass, so housebreaking was practically automatic.

Joker liked his supper and was soon ready for bedtime. How would that work? Would he be lonesome? I lined a cardboard box with a soft sweater, added a wiggly hot water bottle and a small clock, in the hope that the warmth and the tick-tock would lull him to sleep. The result was perfect. After due investigation, he settled happily as expected. I put the box close beside my bed, and for the moment all was serene. I gloated over him a bit, admired him as he slept, then prepared myself for bed and turned off the lights. Scarcely had I gone to sleep when I was awakened by faint cries and scratching on the side of the box. Exactly what I had hoped was happening. So I took Joker into my bed, where he snuggled under my chin, and the pattern was complete. No more clocks or hot water bottles!

From day one we realized that we had a very clever little dog, and he knew that he had already trained three people to make him number one in their lives. When anyone spoke to him he looked at them intently, and we often wondered just how much he really did understand.

We had a clock in the upstairs hall that struck at fifteen-minute intervals. Joker was fascinated by that. He would listen carefully, turning his head from side to side. He soon understood that seven strokes meant it was time to rise and shine, and four strokes was the signal for somebody to go and get the cook. When I came home every day, Joker talked to me at great length, presumably about all the events of his day.

Joker was developing. He was obedient in every way, but he did have some likes and dislikes. We all noticed that one ear drooped; it did not match the other, which was pointed and stood straight up. One morning after breakfast I took him close beside me on the sofa, talked to him softly, and stroked his ear. At first he did not approve of the treatment, but after a few minutes he decided it was not so bad. I planned to continue the routine each morning, and it was a joy that after about three days he would be on the sofa first, awaiting my tender loving care. Soon he would flip both ears as if to say "enough," but in about three weeks when he shook his head, the weak ear responded and stood up to match the other one. He was so very proud, and ever after, in any crisis, Joker came to me as if to say "Mama fix it!"

Then we noticed something else. Joker's tail had grown longer—it had even become a little bushy—and now it formed a perfect circle. It was a perfect doughnut tail! And it wagged almost all his waking hours. Also, he learned to love his leash, which we hung on a hook in the entrance way. He developed the idea of coaxing us to take him for a walk by jingling the harness. How could we refuse? Later, when he was older and my cousin from Chicago spent his winters here, Joker taught him the joys of walking, and together they had several trips each day up and down the sidewalk.

My house is a two-story building with fourteen carpeted steps to the second floor. Joker climbed the steps at his first attempt, but the descent was something else. He was scared. He would sit at the top and whine, sometimes even venturing a bark as he protested his predicament. For days I tried to think of a solution. Joker was smart, but he was terrified of the stairs, and force was not the answer. Then I had an idea. Maybe one step at a time, then two, and so on, and eventually he'd get down the stairs. So I would sit at the bottom of the stairs and coax him to jump off one step, then another, then another. It must have taken two weeks of patience before he forgot his fear and ran downstairs with complete assurance.

Our English professor was assigned a great deal of reading. He was usually home by mid-afternoon, and because he liked the outdoors it was his practice to take a blanket and a glass of ginger ale and lie on the back lawn to read. Joker was always ready to keep him company, and if the glass of ginger ale was at his level, he would try for a taste. The bubbles made him sneeze and sneeze, but he was always ready to try again. Since sharing the same glass was not acceptable, we tried putting a little ginger ale on a saucer for him. The result was much the same, until Joker tried putting his foot on the edge of the dish, tipping it a little. This helped Joker get it down, and from then on he enjoyed his servings to the last drop. Smart, eh?

But more than anything else, Joker loved the car. In fact, "car" might have been the first word he ever really understood. One day, when he was left alone briefly in the car, he decided to let us understand that he did not approve of being left behind. He looked for trouble, and found it in a box of Kleenex, which he emptied piece by piece. When we returned, both the front seat and the back seat were full of Kleenex, and our doggie was exhausted. Probably in his excitement he ran out of breath as he pulled at the tissue and panted. The paper had stuck to his nose, and was in his mouth as well. But Joker must have learned his lesson, for he never repeated that trick again.

The next notable car incident occurred during strawberry season, when Joker managed to open a package of fresh, ripe berries and help himself to the fruit. I'm sure he found them as delicious as we would have! After that we had to transport our strawberries in the trunk of the car, but it didn't fool the dog. From his perch in the back window above the trunk, he would scratch as though he would tear the car apart.

A true car buff, Joker fell in love with the gas station attendant. Sometimes Jim would have a treat for Joker, but not always. In any case, as soon as we pulled in to the gas station Joker would climb up onto the ledge by an open window and crawl out and along the side of the car, to sit on the trunk lid and watch Jim fill the tank. Then one day, when Joker had put on a little weight, he fell while trying to crawl to his ringside seat. He wasn't hurt, but he was embarrassed, and there were no repeat performances after that.

By then Joker was about three months old. He was responding very well to the learning process, but he had figured out that with a little trickery he could get his own way. As we trained him, he trained us. Until then we had never left him in the house unattended; he was still full of puppyish mischief and could not be trusted completely. We found a large cardboard box at the supermarket, its sides high enough to keep Joker inside, and we called it Joker's playpen. As far as he was concerned, however, it was just a plain box.

One Sunday we were all getting ready to go to church, and so we brought Joker's playpen into the kitchen. In one corner we anchored a dish of water, and we also put a pillow, some toys, and some doggie treats into the box. Joker eyed the box hatefully and immediately wanted to go outside. I let him out, but a few minutes later he appeared at the door, walking on his front legs and dragging his hind legs behind him. He was obviously in pain. I gathered him in my arms, and we all examined him together. I was certain he had been struck by a bicycle. I decided to stay home from church to tend to Joker, and the men agreed not to leave us alone. We watched Joker's every movement. In a few minutes, a cat appeared in the back yard. All of a sudden Joker's "pain" disappeared; his eyes widened, and he leaped from the sofa and dashed barking to the door, with no sign of disability. He wanted to show that cat who was boss of the yard.

I was reluctant to admit that Joker had been faking injury—and that it had worked. But the following Sunday he gave exactly the same performance. This time he didn't fool us, though, and we went to church anyway. But when we got back and Joker heard the garage door open, he ran to give us our usual royal welcome. All was forgiven, and there were no further repeats of this particular stunt.

Then came Old Spanish Days, when all of Santa Barbara stops everything to celebrate the Spanish heritage of our city. The historic parade was scheduled for Friday afternoon, and I decided to take Joker along to show him to some friends I was meeting. By this time Joker had learned to walk on a leash very properly, and at the parade he attracted almost as much attention as the beautiful horses and costumed riders.

My car was parked a few blocks away, but Joker and I were both good walkers and didn't mind hoofing it, stopping several times along the way to talk to his admirers. But Joker also kept stopping to scratch. Again and again he'd stop and scratch furiously, then proceed only to stop again a moment later. Finally he became so irritated that he seemed to be pleading with me to make it better somehow. I became so alarmed that I took him straight to the pet hospital to ask advice. The vet was very amused. He sprayed Joker gently with something, rubbed him carefully, and then shook him over the examining table. To my surprise, all sorts of live and dead insects kept falling off the dog. They were fleas, and Joker had apparently picked them up while walking along the sidewalk at the parade. I had never seen a flea before. In the cold climate I had come from, there were no fleas; they must have frozen during the winter months. But here were hundreds of them! Fortunately the vet was able to recommend a remedy, and we were free of fleas in the future.

Shortly thereafter, the house next door to us was sold, and one day I noticed new neighbors moving in. From our upstairs window I could look down into their yard, where I noticed a small gray poodle playing. I called Joker and held him up to the window to see, and he immediately spotted his new friend-to-be, Tuffy. We went downstairs and the two dogs talked through the fence for a while; then suddenly they both began to dig. They became friends instantly, and whichever dog was out first in the morning dug the hole for the day. They spent many happy hours romping and playing together, and their people became good friends too.

Joker soon grew up. He mastered all the basics of good behavior. He had all his puppy shots and was ready to venture into a world of strangers as well as friends. Let us begin at home in familiar surroundings: He knew that the doorbell meant that someone was coming, and he appointed himself the head of the welcoming committee. Very soon he accidentally ruined a lady's stockings as he jumped to greet her, so we had to plan a better way. The stairs in my house are directly in front of the entrance, so I taught Joker to run up the steps, put his head through the posts of the bannister at eye level to most adults, where he could greet guests with a kiss, if they let him. A very successful arrangement!

Once, when we were in the pet section of the Farmers' Market in Los Angeles, one of our group spied a gentleman's collar and bow tie for small dogs. Joker was more excited than I was, and he preferred to wear it day and night. He soon learned, however, that it was for special occasions, for he saw me wrap it and place it carefully with his other treasures. But if we were expecting guests, I would dress him in his "Sunday best," and Joker, feeling important, would go to the next door neighbors' to show off a bit. This soon became standard procedure, much to the amusement of all.

Our neighbors had a standard poodle named Buttons, and the two dogs were together much of the time. Joker often stayed there if I was away from home, sometimes even overnight. One day Buttons was missing. The mother and little daughter of that household were distraught, and tears flowed freely all day. The local radio and television stations and the Humane Society were all contacted, but there was no sign of the missing dog. About eleven o'clock that night I let Joker out for his night run, and he was gone so long that I began to wonder where he was. Finally I heard a commotion at the front door, not at the back door, where Joker usually entered. I went to check, and there stood Joker and Buttons, both soaking wet and covered with mud, but safe and sound and seeking shelter with me. I grabbed Buttons in my arms, and together Joker and I took him home. What rejoicing! We never knew what had happened, but we figured that Buttons had somehow crossed a creek nearby and could not find his way home. After both dogs were thoroughly scrubbed, we hailed Joker as "Hero of the Day." We often wished we knew how and where they had found each other.

Another time we took Joker to the lawn bowling club, where two of us were ardent members. Joker never seemed to make an enemy, and soon he knew the members—the men especially—at the club and where they left their bowling cases while they were playing. Someone found out that Joker liked jerky, and once the news spread many members provided treats. Joker soon knew who these were, and invariably would be found sitting beside jerky-laden bowling cases when their owners returned. It was not long before Joker knew everyone in the club, and if a visitor appeared on the scene, he would bark as if to say, "Have you paid your dues yet?"

One day, in his excitement to greet a friend, Joker jumped from the sidelines onto the bowling green. One of the members picked him up, gave him a light spank, and put him off the grass. Joker's pride was hurt. One lesson was enough; he never made that mistake again.

MacKenzie Park's new bowling green was opened for sport, and Joker was chosen as the mascot. His framed picture, compete with a brass nameplate, hung in the club-house until he died. He went with us to many tournaments and was widely known, even among bowlers from Los Angeles to Vancouver, where he was recognized at the National Tournament.

We had many friends at the bowling green, but one couple surpassed all others and gave me a Christmas memory I will always treasure. On my day off from work, Joker announced with a happy bark that the postman was approaching. They were good buddies, and I let Joker out to greet his friend.

"Joker," said the mailman, "I have a parcel for you." Sure enough, all wrapped up in fancy paper was a package addressed to Joker himself. Naturally, he took it proudly and carried it inside, where we all gathered round. Joker sniffed the package, tugged at the wrapping, and after great effort and cheers from the spectators, opened it. To his satisfaction, it was several days' supply of jerky! We all applauded his fortune.

Sometimes we had anxious moments too. We were leaving the bowling green one day, with the normal chit-chat, plans for future games, and so on; everyone was leaving at about the same time, but we were among the last to say our farewells. When we were about two miles along on the way home, I suddenly missed Joker. We were astounded and could not believe we had left him alone at the park. As quickly as we could, we turned around and went back. But where should we look? Where could he have hidden? Might someone have taken him away?

Remember, I said Joker was smart. He had chosen to wait for us at the gate on the highest ground, so that he could see both ways, and when he saw our car drive in, he came as fast as his four little legs could carry him.

Soon, however, a change was to come that would affect many people—and Joker as well. The man next door, by now a very good friend, was hired as the new administrator of a retirement complex of about three hundred people. He approached me about a job as the first activity director there, and I was tempted. I talked it over with my two doctor employers, and they released me with their blessing, as they wanted me to "work with people rather than with paper."

Where did Joker fit in? Let me relate that I have often wished I had a memory like his and that he could have expressed himself other than by constantly wagging his doughnut tail. After I had a few days of orientation, I took Joker to work with me, where he would meet some new friends.

One day we were walking through the area where the residents lived, and Joker suddenly stopped dead still. He tried in his way to explain to me what he had discovered. Then I understood. One of his bowling pals lived there with his blind wife. Since that man knew about Joker's appetite for jerky, Joker made regular visits there on his own, much to the pleasure and admiration of the blind lady. Joker's call was the highlight of her day.

There was another resident who often sunned herself in the main lounge in the mornings. She had been in the diplomatic service in many parts of the world and had always wished she could have a pet. Joker was the answer to her prayers. He checked that particular place on the sofa every time he visited with me. He knew exactly where he would find her. She lived to be well over one hundred years of age, and one day, long after I had retired and Joker was no longer among us, she told me that when I visited her she often could not remember my name; but she would never forget Joker's.

Of course, Joker knew the administrator of the retirement complex, who was our neighbor. One morning when Joker was with me, we entered the lobby and I heard the administrator laugh. His office was down the hall and in one of the private rooms. Joker stopped and listened. He recognized the voice and took off at full speed to say good morning to his friend. I followed, and I'll always remember that man excusing himself from a telephone conversation, saying, "Hang on a minute. I have to say hello to my neighbor's dog."

Joker even explored the elevator at the retirement center: someone pushed the button, and he found himself having a solo flight. The elevator stopped at the kitchen/dining room level, much to the surprise of the would-be passenger. But the food service manager knew Joker, greeted him with a big hug, and returned him to me on the ground floor.

When Halloween came we had a party for all the residents, many of whom came in costume. I dressed as the Queen of Hearts, with Joker leading the parade on his leash and dressed in a sun bonnet and breeches. He was a smash hit and continued to make more friends for me among so many strangers.

On Saturdays I delivered the mail to the residents in the personal care and skilled nursing facilities. In the second-floor corner apartment of one of the buildings, a retired doctor and his wife lived comfortably. The man was

the victim of a severe stroke and could neither speak nor walk. I was told that about an hour before I was expected, just in case I might be early, he would station himself at the window so that he would not miss a minute of watching Joker approach. Every bit of time was precious to him. As soon as we entered, he would pat his knee with his good hand, and Joker would immediately sit down close by him and be petted for all the time I could spare. As a farewell, Joker always gave the doctor a big lick—as much as to say, "Yes, I like you, too."

But Joker had already achieved a dog's normal lifespan. He had enjoyed every minute of his lifetime, never needed correction, and was never cross or disgruntled. But now he began to slow down. Sometimes when we were walking he would sit down for a few minutes to rest. Sometimes I would have to carry him. Both our wonderful vet and I realized that Joker's heart was weakening, and before long his spells became more frequent and more painful. I gradually understood that Joker really did not want to live any longer. We made an appointment at the animal hospital, and I took him in my arms and kissed him. He returned my goodbye by licking my teary eyes. The vet administered the painless needle, and Joker was gone. He was cremated and placed in the Santa Barbara Humane Society Memorial Garden, where he would join others who had given their best to appreciative masters.

Sparky

IT HAS BEEN SAID that a house is not a home without a dog. After losing Joker, that saying seemed to make sense to me. But where would I start? I telephoned the people from whom I had bought Joker to see if they had any more puppies. No, they said, they didn't have any; but some neighbors of theirs had two pups all ready to go to new homes. I immediately called these neighbors, and the lady informed me that she was preparing to drive to Santa Barbara very soon, and she promised to bring both puppies along.

I went to work at the retirement home the day the woman and her pups were to arrive, and I knew there would be plenty of interest among the residents and staff. In the middle of the day the woman arrived as promised, bearing twin chihuahuas. They were tiny, weighing about one and a half pounds each. One was white with black spots, and the other white with brown spots. They were already named Sparky and Spot. I played with them both for a few minutes; they were both already good pets, so it was just a matter of which I would prefer. The white-and-black one, Sparky, had big eyes, large pointed ears, and a wagging tail, and so without hesitation I chose him to be the next addition to my family.

I immediately noticed that Sparky was very independent. He busied himself checking out his surroundings, and I could hardly wait to take him home. He needed no introduction to an automobile, but accepted my Oldsmobile as a satisfactory conveyance no matter where we might be going. When we got home, I had a chance to examine him more closely. His thin hair was very silky, and the black spots were on his pink skin as well as in his hair. As he had done at the retirement residence, Sparky checked out the situation, then, after a dog biscuit and a drink of water, he found a chair that just suited him for a nap. He settled in like he had always lived there, and almost no get-acquainted period was necessary.

Sparky was fascinated by the stairs. He was very sure on his feet, and he ran up and down the stairs until he was out of breath. Then he discovered a golf ball, which was just his size and proved to be his very favorite possession of all time.

One evening I was to preside over a program at work, and I took Sparky along. The residents were delighted, and Sparky minded his manners very well.

Afterwards, there was a concert that night at the church I attended, and some of my friends wanted me to go with them. I did, but it was too cold to leave Sparky in the car. We decided to take him into the church, wrapped in the blanket I used to carry him around outdoors, on account of his thin hair. The concert had already begun when we arrived, so we eased ourselves into seats in the back row. A couple turned around to see who was coming, and I'll bet they were surprised to see me with my little bundle of joy. The concert proceeded, and all was well until a section came that involved loud music and crashing cymbals. Sparky roused himself, gave two very loud barks, then settled down again; he was not in the least alarmed as long as he remained safely wrapped up in the blanket.

But something was wrong with Sparky, as became clear in the following days. He had trouble eating, although he kept at it until all his food was gone. Sometimes he would put his foot in his mouth and even whine a little. When I saw him on his back on the floor with both front feet in his mouth, I knew it was time to investigate. I was aghast at what I found: Sparky had two complete sets of teeth! His puppy teeth had not fallen out, as they should have when his adult teeth came in. No wonder he was troubled! His mouth was just too full—and very sore.

So off we went to the animal hospital. My trusty vet had never seen such a thing, but knew just what to do. He gave Sparky complete anesthesia and then pulled all of his puppy teeth. I was glad the doctor knew which teeth to pull; they all looked alike to me.

Sparky had a tender mouth for many days, but he enjoyed ice cream whenever he could persuade me with his "Please, Mama."

As I said before, Sparky was very much an individual. He did not want to play with other dogs. On the contrary, he would amuse himself with the least of toys; that golf ball was all he needed most of the time, and he developed his own technique with it. Have you ever seen a person prepare for a shot at billiards? That's how Sparky was with his golf ball. He would take the ball to the landing at the top of the stairs, push it around until he had it in exactly the right position, then push it off with his nose and run down the stairs to catch it at the bottom. Of course, the ball didn't always go straight down the stairs, no matter how carefully Sparky set it up. Once in a while it would go a bit sideways, through the railing, and down onto the floor below. Then Sparky would make all kinds of sounds, which we were never able to interpret. But he would stay in the same place and try to improve his pattern, until he decided to stretch out beside the ball and have a nap.

Another pastime Sparky enjoyed, but tired of more quickly, had to do with the toilet paper in the downstairs bathroom. The distance from the paper holder in the bathroom, through the kitchen, to the living room door is about thirty feet, according to my measurement, and Sparky's challenge was to unroll the paper all that way without breaking it. This he sometimes accomplished by pulling slowly and carefully on the paper; but if it tore before he reached his destination, he would bark loudly to let everyone know that he had tried and failed.

Sparky was a little shy, but he enjoyed people and their kindness to him. My dogs had always been the attraction at whatever parties they attended, and with Christmas approaching I decided to take Sparky to the retirement home for Christmas Eve. He stole the show! When he saw the Christmas tree with its myriad colored lights, he got very excited and his eyes grew bigger and bigger and bigger—a sight many of us would remember for a long time. I had a Christmas stocking that he fit into perfectly, and he was passed around in it from one admirer to another, even posing for a photo for some future Christmas card. He was a real treasure, and I was very proud of the way he accepted all the attention.

•

But Sparky was not always so sociable. One day some guests at my house were in the back yard having a chat with the neighbors; Sparky was amusing himself as usual when from out of the blue another neighbor's big Persian cat appeared and jumped on my little dog. Maybe the cat thought Sparky was a rat and intended to kill him. She certainly tried! Our neighbor ran to help, and someone threw a lawn sprinkler at the fighting animals, hoping to scare the cat off. But the missile hit Sparky, who thought it had been thrown by the neighbor, whom he now turned on and tried to bite. He was scared to death! After that his disposition was spoiled; whenever he spied that particular neighbor he would run for his life. In fact, he was scared of almost everyone.

It was a real test for me to know what to do. I was afraid to take Sparky anywhere, because if anything startled him he would go on the defensive and snap and growl viciously. Finally, after several months of trial and error, it seemed that my love and patience were winning. Sparky had learned to trust me completely, although he was still hesitant about anyone else.

Then there was an accident, and Sparky was severely injured. Despite the best efforts of two veterinarians, hours of surgery, and days of constant care with reports every six hours, Sparky did not make it.

I was devastated. I had friends in town from Vancouver, who were wintering in Santa Barbara, and they came over to try to console me with dinner and a game of bridge. Everyone was so thoughtful of me in my anxiety. But I realized that the only solution would be to find a replacement for my beloved pet—and one came more quickly than I ever could have imagined.

The very next morning one of my Canadian friends

went to the laundromat to do the week's wash. While he was there, a disabled veteran came to do the same. He was holding one hand under his chin, as if to protect something there.

"What do you have under your shirt?" my friend asked him.

The veteran replied, "I have a little pup."

"Is it for sale?" inquired my friend.

"Yes, and no. I want to sell him, but first I want to be sure he has a good home."

"Well, you've found it," said my friend. "Give me your telephone number, and your pup will have the best home in Santa Barbara."

And so information was exchanged, and we made a date to meet the veteran the next day at the laundromat. We made a deal and a promise, and a tiny black puppy was traded from under one chin to under another.

Cupid

THE ARRIVAL OF THIS particular puppy was truly unusual. Who would ever expect to find such a precious pet at a laundromat, of all places? She was truly "heaven sent," and I was part of the plan.

After all the business at the laundromat was transacted and farewells, thanks, and good wishes were exchanged, we took No-Name Puppy directly to the animal hospital for a check-up. As soon as we entered the waiting room we were greeted with "oohs" and "ahhs" from all the office staff. My favorite vet came to see what all the commotion was about. He took the puppy in his arms and assured her she had nothing to worry about in her future. Then he took her to the examining room, where he weighed her—only nine ounces! He described her as a chihuahua-poodle mix, with soft, woolly black hair and a white spot on her chest that extended up to under her chin. She had droopy ears, a very short nose, and a rounded pink tongue. After the examination he wished us both happy years together and suggested that we return for her first shots as soon as she tipped the scales at the one-pound mark.

The waiting room was full of other patients and their people as we left, and again little No-Name aroused much attention. One woman had a suggestion for us: "Since it's February 14," she said, "are you going to name her Valentine?" I paused for a moment to think about it, but Valentine didn't sound like a dog's name to me. "But how about Cupid?" I suggested. The consensus was unanimous. Everyone joined in the applause, and my new pet was named Cupid on the spot with no further discussion.

When we got home I took my new baby dog to meet our neighbors and their large, black standard poodle, Gigi. What a pair they made—one large and one small, but both black and each intensely interested in the other. They made friends immediately, and Gigi became Cupid's guardian. Cupid seemed to like the entire family next door, and as long as she lived she thought she had two homes. She visited the neighbors whenever she liked, and even stayed all night sometimes.

Cupid loved to cuddle. Evidently the veteran from whom I had bought her must have had her sleep with him, for now she turned to me at bedtime. She would say her "goodnights," then snuggle under the covers close to my body. But when I made my very first move in the morning, Cupid was already waiting for me. Immediately she was up to greet me with the kisses she had been keeping for that very special moment.

Cupid lived up to her name. She loved everyone, feared no one, and brought happiness wherever she went. When she especially wanted attention, she would stare at whomever was at hand with her bright, beady eyes and she would smile, showing her pearly white teeth with her tongue outlining her lips. As she grew a little older, straggly black hair covered her entire body, and sometimes she could scarcely see because of the long hair covering her eyes.

I had never owned a dog that liked to have its toenails trimmed—that is, not until Cupid. When she was very young her toenails were sharp and scratchy, and one day I took the clippers in hand to see what I could do about them. Hesitatingly I picked her up, turned her tummy-side up over my knees, and let her sniff the clippers I was about to use. She did not seem to object, so I carefully snipped one, two, three, and four feet with no reaction from Cupid except intense interest in the procedure. After that there was never a problem. If she saw me with the clippers she would turn herself upside down on my lap and wait for her pedicure like it was a special treat.

Cupid did have one bad habit, however: She loved to upset her water dish, and the more water that was in it, the better. At first I thought she only did so to tell me the dish needed filling, but it was not so. She seemed to delight in her trick the most when the dish was full and water sloshed all over the floor. One day, while we were on a trip out of town with friends, I saw a pet shop and decided to see what they could offer in the way of water dishes. We all had opinions. Some thought the ones with short legs and rubber suction cups would be the answer; but to me they seemed too cumbersome for a small dog. I took the one I favored to the cashier and explained that I was buying this one because my pet insisted on spilling water. But he said I should have another kind, and he dashed off to bring the one we had looked at earlier. Since he was so sure, I bought the one he suggested, and we left for home.

At home I scrubbed the new dish, filled it with water, and placed it in the usual spot on the floor. We all went to the living room and left Cupid to examine her new "toy" in private. Soon, to our dismay, she appeared in the living room, carrying the dish in her mouth by one of its legs and with a trail of water all the way back to the kitchen. She did not approve, but she finally accepted the new dish.

Sometimes during hot weather I would put an ice cube in the dish to cool the water. But that was too much for Cupid, who would carefully remove the ice cube before she took her drink.

When Cupid's first teeth began to fall out in readiness for the new ones that would follow, Cupid would bring the fallen teeth to me as though they were treasures to be preserved. Maybe someone had whispered to her about the tooth fairy!

Cupid's own idea of preparedness was having about four dog biscuits cached at strategic locations throughout the house. Usually one could be found behind the living room sofa, one upstairs in a corner behind a bathroom door, and one on the next-to-highest stair step, also tucked into the corner. In addition, there were usually various others stashed in special places here and there. Now, a visiting friend of mine from Ontario did not approve of dog biscuits except in the dog's dish, and she took action to enforce a change. Without comment or notice, biscuits would find their way back to Cupid's dish.

For a while Cupid merely eyed these tricks from her cushion on the sofa; but one day she decided she could not put up with this interference any longer. Her pattern had been disturbed. She boldly arose from where she had been resting, made sure she was seeing right—yes, there was a biscuit in her dish—then glowered at my friend before jumping down to take the biscuit in her mouth and restore it to its proper place in the corner of the same stair step on which it had been found. I watched the proceedings and then said to my friend, "Well, did you get the message?"

Thunderstorms are rare in Santa Barbara, but they do occur. One day, when I was weeding in my garden and Cupid was visiting next door, there suddenly came a loud clap of thunder and a flash of lightning, completely without warning. This was quite new to Cupid, and she let the neighbors know that she wanted to go home right away. She left at high speed, and just then there came another clap of thunder and another flash of lightning. I dropped my weeding trowel as Cupid leaped into my arms, and we hurried into the house as the storm persisted. It was the only time I ever saw Cupid truly scared. Luckily, it was the only such storm we had during Cupid's life; but the incident let us know without a doubt where Cupid felt she truly belonged—at our house, not the neighbors'.

One time my cousins from Ottawa, Canada, were spending some holidays at my house, and I wanted them to meet two couples who were friends of mine. I invited them, and a date was set. When they arrived Cupid was at the neighbors', so she missed hearing the car doors and participating in the greeting. We were all sitting in the living room when Cupid, who must have finally heard the voices, came galloping home at full speed. She stopped at the door of the living room, then proceeded to go around the circle of chairs, stopping in front of each visitor to bark once. With a little imagination we could easily translate her barks as "Hello!" and "Welcome!" Then we were all friends together.

Cupid and I had some friends in care centers, and Cupid understood as well as anyone that these people needed tenderness. She was ready to provide it. They welcomed us both, and Cupid would snuggle up beside them in their beds, and if they petted her she would respond with a gentle lick. Then she would pretend to fall asleep. At one private residence we visited, Cupid would always rush in as soon as the door was open and go straight to the candy dish that sat on a coffee table nearby. Sure enough, her wish would be granted! Her memory served her well.

In one of the homes we visited often, there lived a blind lady who was a devoted dog-lover. She had been an artist in better days, and she prided herself especially on her portraits of dogs. When we were to go to that home, I would phone ahead so that the woman would be in her big easy chair with space beside her ready for Cupid's visit. She would pet Cupid and examine her carefully, then express regret that she could not do Cupid's portrait. One day, as we were leaving after a visit, I mentioned that I would try to be back the next month. Quick of wit, she responded, "If you cannot come, just send the darling dog."

I have a bridge friend who lives at a retirement complex here, and one night another friend and I were planning to visit her. Cupid was invited too, as she was always a perfect guest, napping on my sweater, since this was one of our colder months. After our game we said our farewells and started for the parking lot, Cupid leading the way. We got in my friend's car and took off, and it was only when we arrived at my house at about eleven o'clock that the driver said, "Where's our little friend?" I glanced at the rear seat, which was empty. "We must have left her in the parking lot!" I stammered.

I suggested that my friend go on home; I would phone our hostess and ask her to look in the parking lot and see if Cupid was anywhere in sight. I would take my own car and drive as fast as the law allowed (or faster) to rescue my pet.

I phoned the hostess, who said she'd go look, but I got

in my car and left immediately. I was worried more than I care to relate, but when I drove into our hostess's parking lot I could see by the car's headlights that she was standing in a sheltered area with Cupid in her arms, the two of them wrapped in a woolen sweater. Thanks be to God! She said that right after my call, she had grabbed a sweater to go out to the parking lot, and when she stepped out the door, to her surprise Cupid was sitting right there waiting for her.

Still, I could hardly figure it out. My friend's building is very large; it has two levels, both of which are accessible from both sides of the building. How Cupid ever knew which level and which door was right, I never knew. I only knew the relief and gratitude we all felt after this safe reunion.

But I must tell you about Cupid's birthday party! Ever since I retired, six of us who worked together for many years have celebrated each other's birthdays together. One of our group mentioned how long it was between birthdays during the first part of the year, and I suggested that we could celebrate Cupid's birthday, Valentine's Day, with dinner at my house.

And so, on February 14, we gathered around my dining room table. Since it seemed that a birthday cake with candles wouldn't really be appropriate, I made boysenberry tarts marked with pastry C's for Cupid, and instead of candles I put toothpicks with little hearts on them for decoration.

When it was time for dessert, I held Cupid on my lap and we sang "Happy Birthday" to her. She smiled her best smile as we sang, her pearly teeth and pink tongue making a striking picture. But best of all was the way she nodded her head to each of us as if to say "Thanks." We were so

pleased we sang the song a second time, with exactly the same results.

One incident will always remain fresh in my mind, even though it may not have been the funniest event in Cupid's life. I was working in the back yard when the telephone rang, and I hurried inside to answer it. Before I could return to my gardening, the front doorbell rang. I went to the door and saw, parked in front of the house, a Humane Society vehicle, familiarly known as the Paddy Wagon, used to pick up stray dogs. The uniformed officer was standing in the doorway with Cupid right next to him wagging her tail in greeting.

"Is that your dog?" the officer asked, pointing to Cupid. I said it was, and he continued, "Do you know that she is to be tied or in a fenced yard?"

"Yes, I do," I admitted, "but she was with me in the back, and when I rushed into the house she probably thought I had gone around to the front."

"Does she have a license?" the officer asked.

"Yes, of course," I said.

"May I see it?" he asked.

I went into the house to get the license, and when I returned, Gigi, the neighbor's dog, had brought her ball and joined our friends.

Gigi should have been in the circus; she could bounce a ball and catch it from any height. Now she was doing her very best to entertain the officer, while Cupid looked on in admiration. The officer smiled a little and said, "Is that your dog, too?"

"No," I answered, "she belongs to my neighbor."

"Does she have a license?" he wanted to know.

I assured him she did. My neighbor did not drive, and had gone with me to license her dog at the same time.

With such an unusual show going on, what else could the officer do but tip his cap and admonish me, "Try to keep them under control."

Cupid was an unusual dog all her life. I cannot remember ever needing to reprimand her. She brought joy to everyone she met. She was well named, for Cupid was the Roman god of love, and my dog was a goddess of love in her own right. She never tired of being loved, and the feeling was always mutual. She even loved the veterinarian, and at the vet's reception desk, she knew what that can in the corner was, and let everyone know how and when she expected her treats.

But inevitably Cupid was getting older. Her shiny black hair began to show streaks of white, and I slowly realized that her movements had become slower. One day about noon I noticed a change in her behavior, so much so that I phoned the animal hospital for an appointment.

When we got there, Cupid didn't want to see the vet, whom she usually loved, but wanted to stay in my arms, which was quite unusual for her. After her examination, the doctor said he could find nothing really wrong with her, but he suggested that I hold her close as much of the time as I could.

That was easy to do, but it didn't last long. Cupid stayed quietly tucked under my chin, giving me a little lick now and again. Then her little heart just stopped, and she left me as quickly and as easily as she had come.

Love may fade, but it never dies. Thanks for the memory, Cupid.

Penny

PENNY WAS A MYSTERY TO ME. Sometimes mysteries happen quickly, and sometimes they take more time. Let me tell you about our mysteries together, Penny's and mine.

I counted all the pets I had loved and lost and decided I was too old to chance outliving another one, so I decided I'd have to be content with memories. But no matter how I tried, I could not find a way to pet a memory.

The Humane Society is located not far from my home, and I already knew some of the attendants there. Quite often I would drive by that area, pause, and go on my way. Then I ventured to stop a few times and meander through the kennels. Luckily, all the dogs there as boarders or for sale were large breeds, and it was easy to leave them and return home, still dissatisfied with my lot.

Then one morning my telephone rang, and a voice said, "Mrs. Elliott, this is the Humane Society calling to say we have your dog."

I was speechless, but silently my heart leaped. I ex-

plained that I still hadn't decided whether or not to get a
new dog, but the woman on the phone was a good sales-
person and suggested that I stop by and see what they
had. My car was being serviced, so I could not go that day,
but the woman assured me they would hold this particular
treasure until the next day.

I had a very restless night trying to make a decision.
Yes, I would like a pet; I wanted one with all my heart.
But what if something happened to me and I had to give
it up? Many more "what if" scenarios came to my mind,
but because I had already promised to go the next day, I
was obliged to keep my appointment.

The receptionists were watching for me, and as soon
as I entered a male employee brought in a black-and-tan
chihuahua-terrier mix, bright and anxious to go somewhere, but sore of body. When the dog saw me, the man
could not hold her. She leaped into my arms with much
whining, and they explained that there was some problem
with one of the dog's ribs. I tried to pass her back to the
attendants, but she would not go. I did not know that an
animal could actually cling to a person, but this dog could.
She would not let go of me. I saw her great need, and I
realized at once that here was my pet number ten.

It is difficult to be glad and sad at the same time. That
was part of the mystery. Even as I took my new pet to the
car, wishing I could examine her touchy spots, I wondered
if I was ready to accept the challenge. But she was mine
now, for better or worse. She was about four years old, and
had been given a name that did not suit a scared little dog.
"How would you like to be called Penny?" I whispered.
Even though she was very ill at ease, she gave me a big
lick, and together we talked and even sang a song about
Penny. She seemed to realize that in her new life she
would be known as Miss Penny Elliott.

For me it was a new experience to have a full-grown dog. Penny had much to learn, and also much to forget. Besides having sore spots on her body, she was still scared, wide eyed and aware of all noises. She never stopped staring at me and I, in turn, observed her carefully. She weighed about seven pounds, had thick short hair as smooth and soft as satin with bits of white mixed in here and there with the black and tan. Her forehead was her crowning jewel: it was actually blocked off in small squares, with colors blended together like mosaic tile work. Her tail was thick, black on the top and light brown underneath, and she carried it straight up when she walked around. Her markings were exact, almost as if traced from a pattern, and her tongue was thin and long. When we saw her pant a little, we wondered if she had to fold up her tongue to put it away. It was very unusual, to say the least.

I soon learned that Penny was not housebroken. Why go outside when she could stop anywhere? Perhaps this had been part of the problem with the couple who had owned her previously. I could never reprimand her, tiny and frightened as she was. But I had another idea: treats! Would she like raisins? We went outside, where the world was much too big and strange for her; but we walked around and as soon as there was a positive result, we would hurry back inside and go to the cupboard and get one raisin. Penny liked that performance, and as soon as she became better acquainted she would go out on her own, do nothing, and then return to sit in front of the cupboard where the raisins were kept—and bark. She really enjoyed raisins. Not just the flavor of them; she also liked to toss them up high into the air and catch them as they came down.

The first night she was with me, Penny slept better

than I did because I was trying to plan ahead. I had a baby blanket that I left where she could rest on it, and very quickly it became hers. In the car, in the house, or even at a friend's house, she felt very secure with her blanket. Later, when she was acquainted with friends and we went to visit, she would wait for me to put her blanket on a chair. Then she'd curl up on the blanket, and she required no more attention until we were homeward bound.

After Penny's first two or three days, when she had learned to manage the stairs, she discovered an "under the bed." Evidently, it had been her former habit to escape to such a refuge, and at the least disturbance she would run up the stairs and under the bed, sometimes peering out through the fringe of the bedspread at the unknown world beyond.

Before the first week had ended, I learned something else. We were walking around in front of the house when in a flash Penny was gone across the street. The reason, it seemed, was that she had heard a man's voice and had gone running to him. Could it be the voice she knew so well from her former life? Therefore I was sure that it had been the lady of her former house who had hurt her, for it was noticeable that she very quickly made friends with men, but she was very dubious of women. She tried this trick of crossing the street a couple more times, but the third time I gave her one gentle spank. She never went across the street again, and that was the one and only time I made her feel the meaning of "no."

Penny had very strong hind legs and could walk upright on them a mile, or so it seemed, either forwards or backwards. She understood that such a performance would attract attention, and so she tried it often, usually when it was least expected.

Another one of her unique pranks was performed

when we were in the garden together. Then Penny would hide behind some plants, and though I would call for her over and over, she wouldn't budge until I had looked and looked, and then she would jump out and run around me in a circle, barking because she had won the game.

Even though my neighbor loved dogs and tried to be Penny's best friend, Penny never accepted her. She would stay at the neighbors' house briefly during the daytime, but never after dark. Maybe my neighbor reminded her of the one who used to punish her for her mistakes and who could forget when they really hurt.

Shortly after Penny came to live with me I gave her an old sweater of mine to play with on the sofa. Every now and then it would be exercise time, and she would pull, tear, unravel, and growl until she was exhausted. Then it was time for a snooze on the perfect pillow she had been able to arrange all by herself. One of my friends was ashamed of that sweater, I think, so she knitted Penny a new toy. It was closely knit, and of tougher yarn, but Penny was now older, stronger, and more determined. It was real entertainment to see how long she would work at dismantling that sweater.

As the prank in the garden proved, Penny liked to play tricks. It was a thrill to me to see her in a playful mood, for I knew I must be doing something right. One day at noon I wanted to watch something in particular on television. I made myself a sandwich and took my TV tray to the sofa. Then I chose a medium-size sweet cucumber pickle and placed it on a saucer on the arm of the sofa. The phone rang, calling me away, and when I returned and sat down to my bit of lunch, I found that although the sandwich was untouched, the whole pickle had disappeared. I looked at Penny. She played shy, rolling her eyes as she often did, as if to tell me where the pickle had gone. Then she licked her lips, ears, and face with the long tongue I mentioned earlier.

Whenever we went visiting, Penny sized up the situation and led me from the parking lot to the house of whomever we were to visit. Usually she knew the way very well, but she would always turn around several times to see if I were following. If our hostess had a special place to keep treats, Penny would take up a vigil in a well-chosen spot and wait—and wait and wait. It was very interesting to watch her plan how to get her way. In some homes she found that the hostess would provide a dish of water for her; but that, too, sometimes required a gentle reminder. Every home was different, but Penny was never confused. She always led the way, and she always got her messages across.

Like my other dogs, Penny always slept beside me in the bed. When she first arrived I had to carry her up the stairs, and that became our ritual. Although she would go up and down the stairs on her own at any other time of day, at bedtime she expected to be carried. If I had something else in my hands and suggested that she come on her own four legs, she would just sit there and eventually start crying, and I had to make a special trip down to get her.

As you can see, Penny was very vocal. She even tried to talk. She had various tones of voice, and she was always watching closely for reactions. When we went to bed, I would turn down the covers, let her jump all over, and then I'd kneel down to talk to her. This was what she loved most, so I suggested we say our prayers together. She would lie down on her tummy with her front legs out straight in front of her and her nose between her feet, and we prayed in call and response.

Our prayers should have been recorded. I would say

one sentence of my prayers; then Penny would say "grrrr..." as if in response, and wait for me to continue. It seemed she was expressing her reverence, too. Finally I would say "amen," and that was her cue to turn around and crawl under the covers, where she would sleep undisturbed until morning. She seemed to understand that "amen" meant the end, and that might well have been the word she knew best of all her vocabulary.

Penny loved my bed, and wouldn't be comfortable anywhere else. Once I nearly had to give up going to a family reunion because of Penny. The reunion of our cousins was to take place in British Columbia. I couldn't take Penny with me; I knew she wouldn't stay with the neighbor overnight; and I was unwilling to board her. So it seemed I could not possibly make the trip. My decision had practically been made when, one Saturday morning, one of my dear friends came by in her car. Penny announced that someone was in our driveway, and we went out together to meet our friend. We chatted a bit; we always had lots to talk about because we had worked together for many years. Then my friend asked me if I had thought any more about going to the reunion, and I told her that I had all but decided not to go—I just couldn't leave Penny alone.

Then, out of the blue sky, my friend made an offer. What if she were to come over and sleep in my bed with Penny while I was gone? What a wonderful offer! So we embraced, perhaps even shed a few tears, and my plans became reality.

As Penny matured and became more sure of herself, I often thought she enjoyed playing the field to see the reaction. Well, she finally did!

Have you ever stopped in front of a mail box in a shopping mall to mail a letter, stepped around to avoid a puddle, deposited the letter in the slot, and turned around to get in the car only to find that all the doors are locked? Well, I did! Add to that disaster that your pet—in my case, Penny—is waiting uneasily in the car, which is still idling, and another car with an irate driver is waiting to park in your spot. Suddenly it was an emergency. Where could I find a phone to call the Automobile Club? Where was my purse? Where were my glasses? Where was my AAA card? Oh, dear!

After much delay I persuaded the AAA representative on the phone that he could find my records on his computer and that I could provide corroborating information such as the make of car, color, and license number. He agreed to dispatch help within forty minutes. I have always been grateful that the delay was shorter than that, because I was cold, and Penny was distressed because she was alone and I was close by but not close enough. She was howling, yelping, and attracting lots of attention from dog lovers, who came from every direction to rescue her from whatever terrible calamity might have befallen her. She soon had quite an audience around her!

One special part of our day was always mealtime. Penny was always ready for samples when we sat down at the table. But first we said grace. When I was alone with her, I taught her to sit quietly at my feet with her head bowed until she heard "amen," that word she knew so well. I tried hard to teach her to close her eyes, but I never succeeded—maybe because she was curious about what was going on around her; I don't know.

Sometimes I had people at my house who are not in the habit of having a blessing before meals, but we said the blessing just the same. Instead of explaining our practice to them, I would merely say softly, "Penny, bow your head." Instantly she would drop her head, and she kept her position until the magic word "amen" was heard. She made many friends with such performances, and taught a few lessons, too.

Ever since retirement I have worked as a volunteer at my church one day a week. As there was no one at home, I took Penny with me. There was a space near my desk, between me and the wall, for a small chair. I would spread Penny's blanket on the chair and she would be dancing to be lifted onto it. And she would stay right there all day.

Penny became acquainted with many church members and friends, and it seemed she had a welcome for everyone. Someone suggested that I teach her to answer the phone. She hadn't been there very long before she noticed that the UPS driver usually came at mid-afternoon and always carried dog biscuits in his pocket. When the time approached, she would stir from her nap and be on the alert facing the door. When the UPS driver came around the corner, she would leap onto my lap, over the top of anything in the way, run to greet him at the door, and coax a biscuit from him. We still talk about her fondly on his regular calls.

All too soon, however, I realized that Penny was losing some of her zip. Her beautiful forehead had turned to the silver tones, but I tried to keep all negative thoughts from my mind. One day I found a tooth in a chair where she had been sleeping. I examined Penny and found that a couple of other teeth were also missing, and over the next weeks I found additional teeth once in a while. We went to the animal hospital, where my faithful vet said Penny could always manage with soft food. He told me not to worry, but I think he had his own ideas.

Then one day I was working outside and Penny came to me. She was moving very, very slowly. With surprise I noticed that her little face was distorted. I thought that one or more teeth must have been loose but still attached, so away we went to the animal hospital, hoping to find a way to relieve her pain.

As soon as we came in and met the vet he took Penny from my arms into his—much against her wishes—and suggested that I return in an hour. But I already knew what he would tell me. When I came back there was no happy greeting. Penny's bones were seriously deteriorated, and her jaw had broken. There was only one course of action to take, and reluctantly I agreed. How could this happen? It was yet another mystery in the life of Penny.

Naturally, I felt that my world had turned upside down. While I was preparing myself to leave the vet's and go out on the street, a little boy about eight years old dashed from the examination area, across the waiting room, and outside. I learned that his dog had been struck by a truck and would not recover. When I reached the parking lot I saw him crying behind a car. I went over and put an arm around him and told him I understood. I asked him what his dog's name was and a few more questions, then I suggested he get a new puppy. He said his mother had told him they would find a new one as soon as possible. Then he asked me about my dog; what had her name been? When I told him her name was Penny, he said, "I like that name. Maybe I'll name my new dog Penny, too."

And so, my Penny will live forever in the hearts and eyes of her readers.

Amen. So may it ever be!

Epilogue—
The Hidden Years

BECAUSE SO MANY PETS have pulled at my heart strings, it seems only fitting to relate some of the highlights from my album of memories.

I was in my teenage years before I ever had a small-breed dog, but being on a farm I found many interests to test my knowledge of animal husbandry.

We always had at least one cat around the barn and in the house. When I was about four years old, I recall, I followed dear Tabby one day and came upon her new family of four squirming, hungry babies, their eyes still tightly closed. I tried to open their eyes, but they were stuck somehow. I went to get warm water and a soft cloth to assist me in my treatment, but when I came back, to my surprise, the kittens were missing. I looked around and saw the mother cat with a kitten in her mouth, carrying it by the scruff of its neck. I tried to rescue it, but its mother became agitated and spat at me. It was several days before I found their new hideaway and, fearing that they would starve to death, I got some warm cow's milk at milking time and tried to feed it to them. But the little kittens did not even know how to drink yet. By the time their eyes were open, their mother drank along with them, and they were quick to follow her example. That was my introduction to feline child-rearing practices.

The next small-animal family I became interested in was baby pigs. No one need ever tell me about "dirty" pigs. If they are given a chance, they can be the cleanest of all animals.

Mother pig had a very large family. She was quite proud of them, and when I appeared she allowed me to hold any one I could catch. They were very pink under their bristly white hair, and greeted me with the happiest of oinks.

Soon it was lunch time. But Mother pig didn't seem to have enough feeding stations for her large family, and each baby had to fight for its right to a turn. When I tried to help, the mama became irritated, and her aggressive oinking let me know that my help was not needed; but I would be welcome to return after nap time.

Then came the little calves—such awkward things, to be sure. Their legs seemed to bend in too many places, and even when I tried to help them stand we had little success. They soon learned to drink from a pail, and as soon as I rattled a pail in their vicinity I had a customer ready. Calves were a lot of fun, and we spent many happy hours together, no one worrying where I might be as we learned to play different kinds of games in the pasture fields.

Our little colts deserve mention, too, of course. My dad informed me that if you gave a newborn colt butter and brown sugar for its first taste of food, it would be your friend for life. He usually planned my arrival at the proper time, and true to his prediction I could go to the pasture field for many months and the colts would canter toward me and sniff and sniff until they found the pocket that contained their treat.

But next to small dogs, I think cows were always my favorite animals. They were so placid—never in a hurry—and so loving with their big, rough tongues. I never did quite understand what it meant when one said a cow was "chewing her cud." What is a cud? Something you could not see; but it gave the cows such a sense of contentment. I knew all our cows by name, and they watched for me and curried my favor. When we gave up the farm and our herd of Holsteins was to be sold at public auction, I went to the stable the night before and, with tears streaming down my face, kissed each one goodbye.

Horses, on the other hand, intimidated me. Colts were okay, but horses were just too big. My dad's first love was horses, and he had raised one, named Britt, from a colt. When my dad opened the stable door in the morning, Britt would whinny—not for anyone else, just for Dad, who then went to Britt's stall and returned his good morning greeting with a pat on the hip.

So, as you see, there are no dumb animals. They merely need kindness to develop their natural traits.

Crossword Puzzle

Contributed by Doug Willsie

Now that you've read about Audrey and her dogs, can you complete the crossword puzzle about them?

Each dog is described by a two-word personality clue.

DOWN

1. Most attentive
2. Most intelligent
5. Sweetest disposition
6. Most clever
8. Most unlucky
12. Author
14. Author's pets

ACROSS

3. Most attentive
4. Everyone's friend
7. Most timid
9. Best "talker"
10. Most kind
11. Most agile
13. Author